ḤANUKAH IN MY HOUSE

by Norma Simon

illustrations by Ayala Gordon

United Synagogue Commission on Jewish Education

חֲנֻכָּה

Copyright © 1960 by United Synagogue of America. Printed in U.S.A.

Hanukah in my house
   is such a happy holiday.
8 nights and 8 days
   of candles in the Menorah,

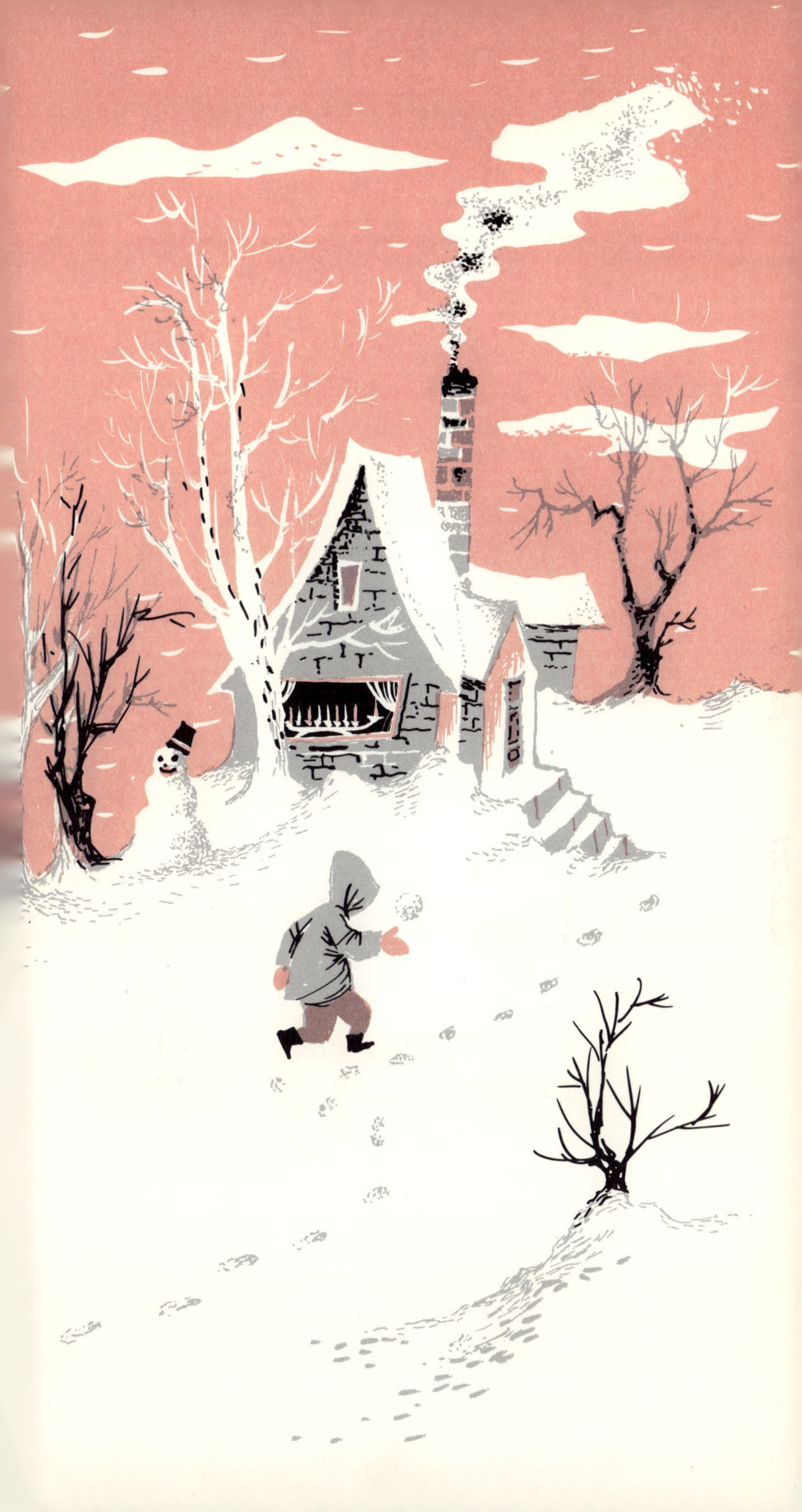

and presents,

and Hanukah *Gelt*,

and *Latkes*,

and *Dreidels* spinning,

and stories of Judah Maccabee.

8 nights and 8 days
of laughing, and singing,
and having a happy time.

Ḥanukah is a happy holiday,
>   a time for extra good treats.

Mother makes potato *Latkes*.

David likes them with applesauce.

I like them with sour cream.

Daddy helps Mother grate white potatoes.

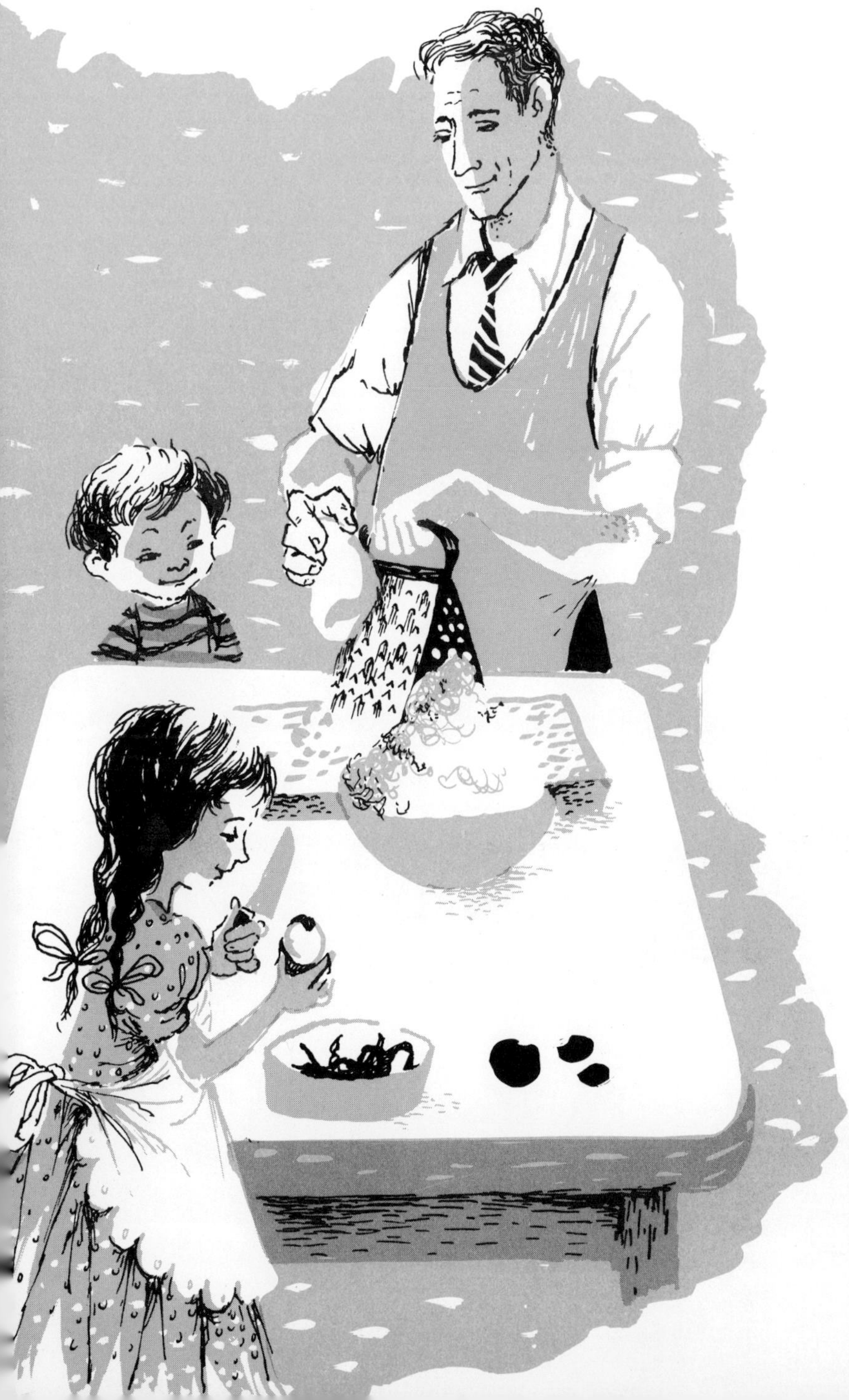

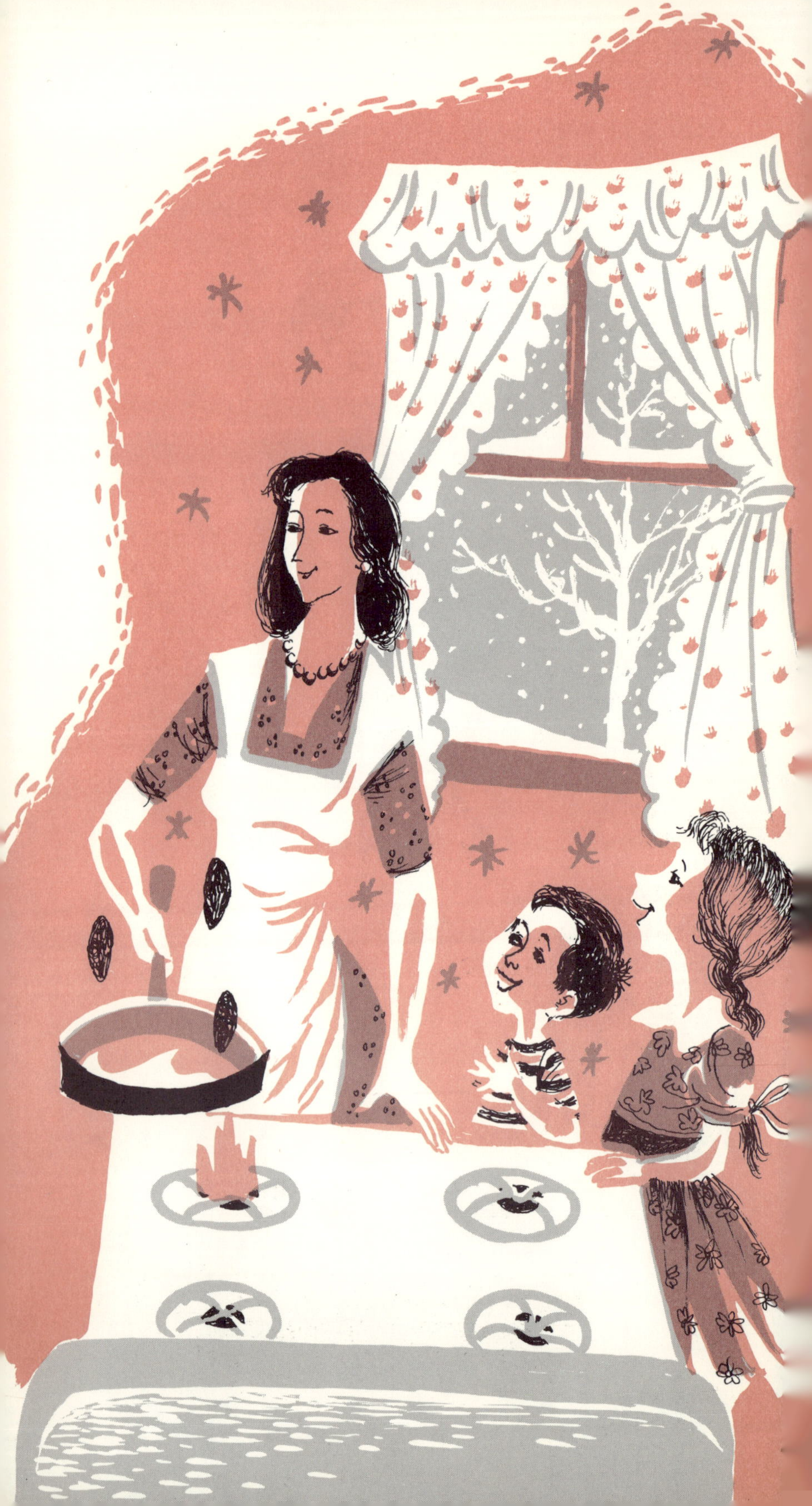

Mother strains out the water,
> makes little patties,
> beats up the eggs,
> heats up the oil,
> drops in the potato patties.

David and I watch them
> sizzle and bubble around the edge.

When the *Latkes* are brown and crusty,
> Mother flips them over.

David smacks his lips.
I smell the *Latke* smell.
We set the table for *Latkes*.

Grandma and Grandpa come.
 Grandma and Grandpa come the 1st night
  to help us light our candles,
  to help us watch our candles burn,
  to give us Ḥanukah *Gelt,*

to watch us open our presents,
to watch us spin our *Dreidels,*
to tell us again about Judah Maccabee,
to help us eat the *Latkes.*

The 1st night the *Shamash* is lit,
and just 1 candle.

The 2nd night the *Shamash* is lit,
and just 2 candles.

The 3rd night the *Shamash* is lit,
and just 3 candles.

The 4th night the *Shamash* is lit,
and just 4 candles.

The 5th night the *Shamash* is lit,
and just 5 candles.

The 6th night the *Shamash* is lit,
and just 6 candles.

The 7th night the *Shamash* is lit,
and just 7 candles.

And the last night the *Shamash* is lit,
and all 8 candles.

And each night we sing the prayer:
Barukh Atah Adonai, Elohenu Melekh Ha-Olam, Asher Kidshanu B'mitzvotav V'tzivanu L'hadlik Ner Shel Ḥanukah.

Daddy gives us Ḥanukah *Gelt*,
  sometimes it's another present.

Every night, for 8 nights and 8 days,
we spin our *Dreidels*,

and sing our Ḥanukah songs.

The song I like best is

Ḥa - nu - kah, Ḥa - nu - kah, hap - py hol - i -

Ḥa - nu - kah, Ḥa - nu - kah, spin the *Drei - del*

a - nu - kah, Ḥa - nu - kah dance and sing so gay.

spin, spin, Spin, spin, spin, Spin the *Drei - del* round.

David and I sing this song.
We spin like the *Dreidels*.
We spin, spin, spin,
    spin, spin, spin,
    spin ourselves around.

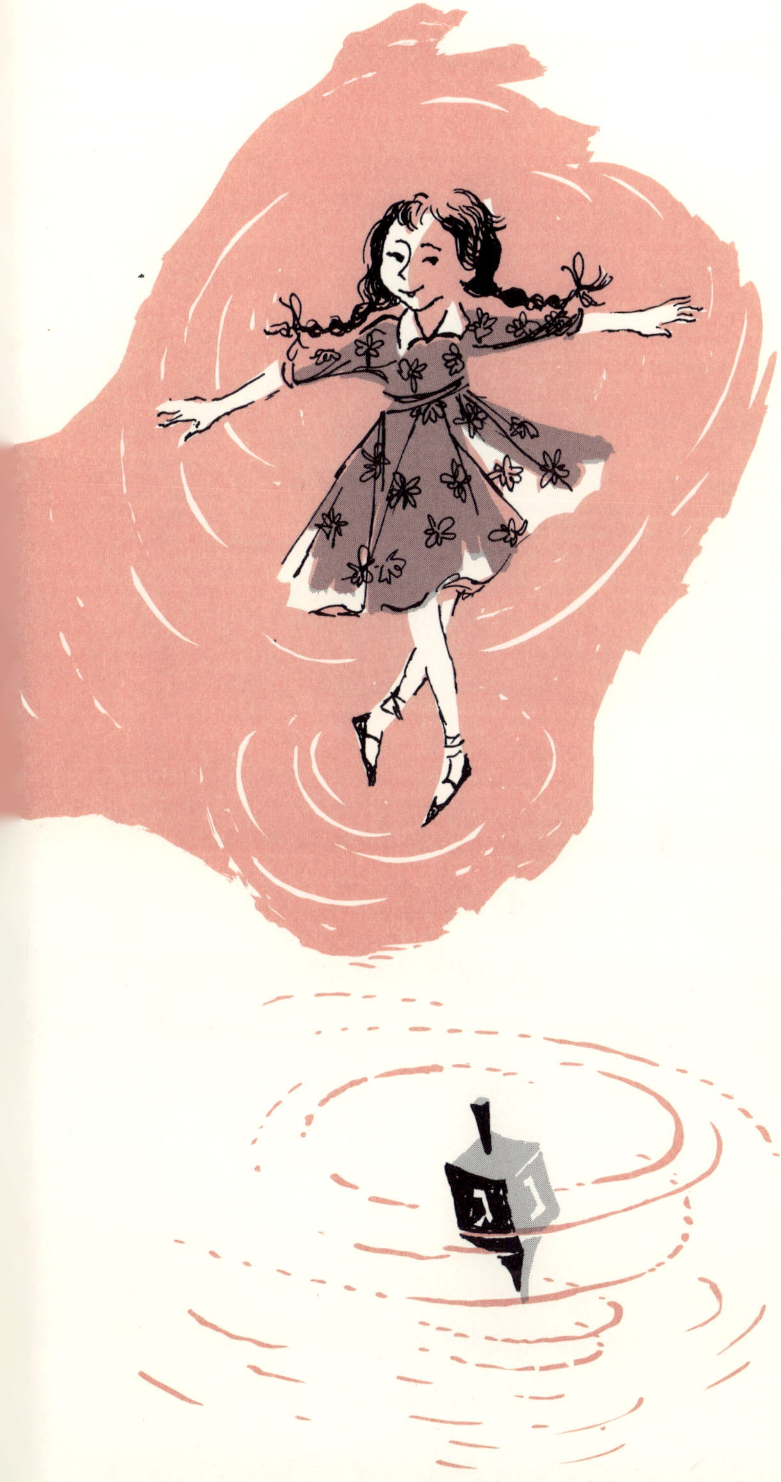

The last night of Ḥanukah,
>the 8th night of Ḥanukah,
>>when the *Shamash* and all the candles are lit
>>we watch them burn down very slowly.
>We know these will be the last of the Ḥanukah
>>>candles,
>>the last of the *Latkes,*
>>the last of the *Dreidels* spinning,

the last of the Ḥanukah *Gelt* and presents,
the last of the nights of Ḥanukah,
and the story of Judah Maccabee,
the last of Ḥanukah
    until next year,
        next winter,
    next Ḥanukah,
        when it will all begin again.

WORDS FOR PRONUNCIATION
AND DEFINITION

Ḥanukah (ḤAH-noo-kah)—The Feast of Lights.
Gelt—Money given as a gift to the children.
Dreidel (DRĀ-dle)—A special spinning top for Ḥanukah.
Latke (LAHT-ke)—Potato pancake, a Ḥanukah delicacy.
Judah Maccabee (MAC-abee)—The leader of the Jewish revolt against the Syrian Greeks.
Shamash (SHAH-mash)—Servant, the candle with which the lights are kindled.
Menorah (M'NŌ-rah)—The candelabrum used for the Ḥanukah lights.